Animal World

Chimpanzees

Donna Bailey and Christine Butterworth

STECK-VAUGHN
L I B R A R Y
A Division of Steck-Vaughn Company

Chimpanzees live together in groups in
the rain forests of Africa.
Each group lives in its own part
of the forest.

A fully grown chimpanzee is about
four feet tall.
It has a thick body and long, strong arms.

A chimpanzee has no fur on its face.
Its ears are the same shape as human ears.

4

A chimpanzee uses its feet and hands
to climb trees.
Its long toes can curl around
to grip branches.

Leopards sometimes climb trees
to kill chimpanzees.
This chimpanzee climbed up to a safe place.
These branches would break if a leopard
tried to climb on them.

The chimpanzee travels quickly and safely through the forest.
It uses its long arms to swing from branch to branch.

Chimpanzees live on the ground,
as well as in trees.
On the ground, a chimpanzee walks
on all fours.
It bends its fingers and walks
on its knuckles.

8

Chimpanzees show how they feel
by making noises.
They also use their faces.
When a chimpanzee is afraid, it pulls back
its lips to show its teeth.

The members of a group of chimpanzees
take care of each other.
They groom each other to keep clean.

Chimpanzees make a lot of noise.

They hoot and mutter.

They shriek and scream and
bang on the branches of the trees.

These chimpanzees have found some fruit.
They hoot and drum their fists on
their chests to let the rest of their group
know that they have found food.

The rest of the group comes running
to enjoy the feast.

Another group of chimpanzees
has heard the noise.
A big male comes to find out what
all the noise is about.

14

The group screams at the stranger.
Their leader throws fruit and stones at him.
He drives the other chimpanzee away.

During the day, a chimpanzee rests
on the ground.
In the evening, the chimpanzee climbs
a tree and makes a nest where it can sleep.

The chimpanzee bends branches over
and weaves them into a flat bed.
Leaves and dry grass go on top.
It only takes ten minutes to make the nest.
Then the chimpanzee can sleep there safely
all night.

A family of chimpanzees has come
down to the river to drink.
First, the big males make sure
there is no danger.

One of the males wades into the river
to get a drink.
Chimpanzees sometimes use leaves
to scoop up water to drink.

Now the rest of the family comes
down to the river.
Can you see a baby chimpanzee
with its mother?

20

The chimpanzee's mother has found
some fruit.
She grunts and bites into the juicy melon.

The baby rushes over to see
what its mother has found.
This tiny chimpanzee is learning how
to swing from branch to branch.

A baby chimpanzee has a lot to learn.
It takes a long time to grow up.
Young chimpanzees learn by copying
the older chimpanzees.

A female chimpanzee has one baby
about every five years.
The newborn chimpanzee holds on to
its mother's fur.
The mother carries her baby around like this
until it is about six months old.

The mother takes care of her baby
all the time.
She holds it in her arms when it
drinks her milk.

This baby is about six months old.
It rides on its mother's back
as she swings through the forest.
It still drinks her milk.

This young chimpanzee is two years old.
It does not need milk now.
It has learned to eat the same food
the adult chimpanzees eat.

The chimpanzees live together in a group.
The mothers help take care of
the babies and young chimps.
They groom each other.

A four-year-old chimpanzee will travel
by itself, but it still stays close
to its mother.
When it is six, the chimpanzee will
live by itself.

Chimpanzees spend most of their day looking for food.
They eat fruit, insects, leaves, and sometimes small animals.

Chimpanzees like to eat ants.

This chimpanzee has found an anthill.

It finds a stick to push inside the hill.

The ants cling to the stick.
Now the chimpanzee can pull out
the stick and lick off the ants.

Index

Africa 2

ants 31, 32

arms 3, 7, 25

baby chimpanzees 20, 22–26, 28

back 26

body 3, 24

branches 5–7, 11, 17

climbing 5, 6, 16

drinking 18, 19

ears 4

face 4, 9

fear 9

feet 5

female chimpanzees 24

fingers 8

food 27, 30

fruit 12, 15, 21, 30

grooming 10, 28

groups 2, 10, 12–15, 28

hands 5

insects 30

knuckles 8

learning 22, 23

leaves 17, 19, 30

leopards 6

lips 9

male chimpanzees 14, 15, 18, 19

milk 25–27

nest 16, 17

noises 9, 11, 12

rain forests 2

teeth 9

toes 5

Reading Consultant: Diana Bentley
Editorial Consultant: Donna Bailey
Executive Editor: Elizabeth Strauss
Project Editor: Becky Ward

Picture research by Jennifer Garratt
Designed by Richard Garratt Design

Photographs
Cover: Bruce Coleman (Kim Taylor)
Bruce Coleman: 4 (Jen & Des Bartlett), 7 (Peter Jackson), 6, 8, 10, 11, 12, 13,
    14, 15, 16, 17, 25, 26, 27, 28, 29, 30 (Helmut Albrecht), 31, 32 (Peter Davey)
OSF Picture Library: title page, 2, 3, 5, 9, 18, 19, 20, 21, 22, 23, 24 (Mike
    Birkhead)

Library of Congress Cataloging-in-Publication Data: Butterworth, Christine.   Chimpanzees / Christine Butterworth
and Donna Bailey.   p.   cm.—(Animal world)   Includes index.   SUMMARY: Highlights the lifestyle and habits of the
chimpanzees of the African rain forests.   ISBN 0-8114-2642-4   1. Chimpanzees—Juvenile literature   2. Social
behavior in animals—Juvenile literature.   [1. Chimpanzees.]   I. Bailey, Donna.   II. Title.   III. Series: Animal world
(Austin, Tex.)   QL737.P96B88   1990   599.88′440451—dc20   90-9928   CIP   AC